Angel Island

by Lori Mortensen

illustrated by Matthew Skeens

只是因为我的家里穷。
只是因为我的国家弱
我为什么坐牢

PICTURE WiNDOW BOOKS
Minneapolis, Minnesota

Special thanks to our advisers for their expertise:

Casey Lee, Interpreter
Angel Island State Park, San Francisco, California

Ling Wang, Ph.D., Lead Teacher of the Chinese Program
Department of Asian Languages and Literature, University of Minnesota, Twin Cities

Terry Flaherty, Ph.D., Professor of English
Minnesota State University, Mankato

Editor: Shelly Lyons
Designer: Abbey Fitzgerald
Page Production: Melissa Kes
Art Director: Nathan Gassman
Associate Managing Editor: Christianne Jones
The illustrations in this book were created digitally.
Photo Credit: Library of Congress, 23

Picture Window Books
151 Good Counsel Drive
P.O. Box 669
Mankato, MN 56002-0669
877-845-8392
www.picturewindowbooks.com

Library of Congress Cataloging-in-Publication Data
Mortensen, Lori, 1955-
Angel Island / by Lori Mortensen ; illustrated by Matthew Skeens.
p. cm. — (American symbols)
Includes index.
ISBN 978-1-4048-4704-0 (library binding)
1. Angel Island (Calif.)—Juvenile literature. 2. Angel Island (Calif.)—History—Juvenile literature.
3. San Francisco Bay Area (Calif.)—History—Juvenile literature. 4. Angel Island Immigration Station
(Calif.)—Juvenile literature. 5. Immigrants—United States—History—Juvenile literature. 6 United States—
Emigration and immigration—History—Juvenile literature. I. Skeens, Matthew, ill. II. Title.
F868.S156M675 2008
979.4'62—dc22   2008006335

Table of Contents

Welcome! My name is Tye. I worked at the Angel Island Immigration Station in San Francisco Bay. About 1 million people passed through Angel Island from 1910 to 1940. For many, it was a difficult journey. Come, and I will tell you how the Angel Island Immigration Station became a symbol of hope for immigrants and their struggle for freedom.

Gateway of the West

Angel Island is in San Francisco Bay, in California. San Francisco was once called the "Gateway of the West." Many people from other countries entered the United States through San Francisco. For many years, immigrants arrived at Angel Island. But getting through the Angel Island Immigration Station was not easy.

Tye Leung Schulze was a real person. She worked as an interpreter at Angel Island in 1910 and was the first Chinese-American to vote.

A Long Journey

During the 1800s and early 1900s, millions of people left their homelands for the United States. They came to escape hard times at home and to make a better life. These people were called immigrants.

Immigrants sailed to San Francisco from countries such as China, Japan, Russia, and India. Journeys often lasted three weeks and covered 7,000 miles (11,200 kilometers). Immigrants with little money traveled in steerage—the bottom of the ship. Steerage was noisy and crowded.

In 1848, gold was discovered in California. As stories of great wealth spread, thousands of people came to California hoping to find gold. Chinese people called California *Gam Saan*, or "Golden Mountain."

Exclusion Laws

Once the gold rush began in 1848, many U.S. citizens were not happy about Chinese immigrants coming to the United States. By the 1870s, gold and jobs became difficult to find. Many U.S. citizens blamed Chinese workers for taking away their jobs and working for less money.

In response, U.S. government officials passed the Chinese Exclusion Laws of 1882. The laws were the first to limit immigrants' entry into the United States based on race. The laws favored middle-class Chinese immigrants. They kept Chinese workers with less money out of the country.

In many western U.S. cities, riots broke out. Angry citizens drove Chinese immigrants out. Chinese people began living in their own communities, called Chinatowns.

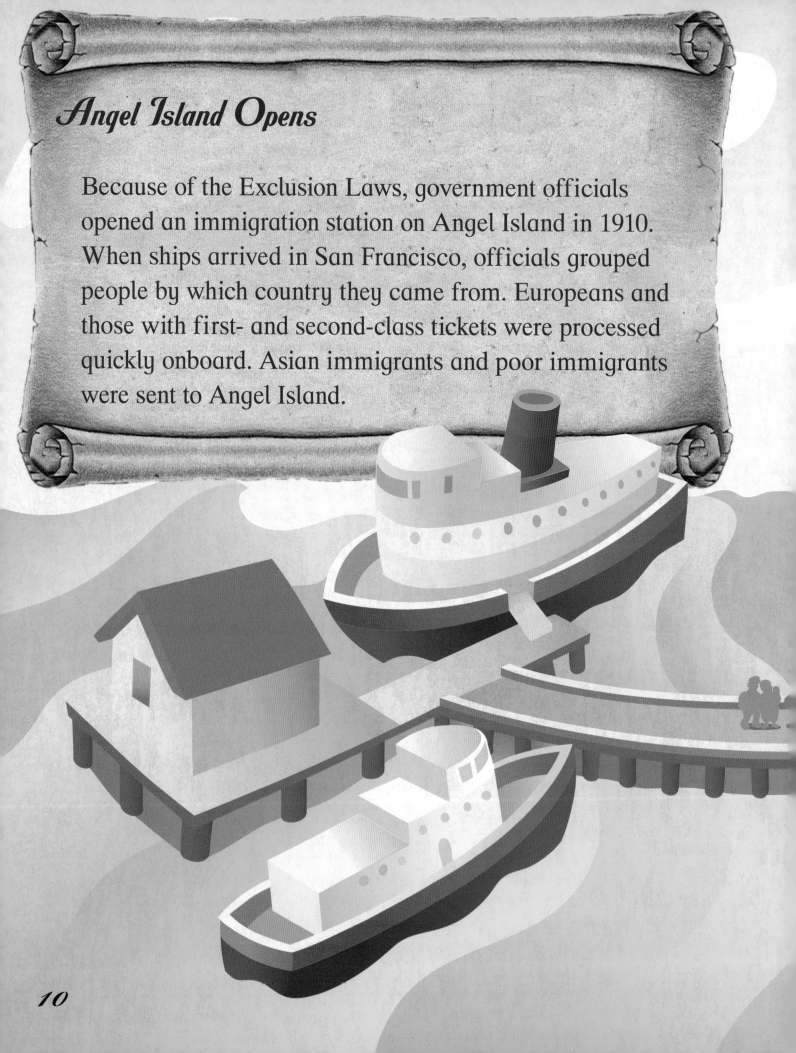

Angel Island Opens

Because of the Exclusion Laws, government officials opened an immigration station on Angel Island in 1910. When ships arrived in San Francisco, officials grouped people by which country they came from. Europeans and those with first- and second-class tickets were processed quickly onboard. Asian immigrants and poor immigrants were sent to Angel Island.

The immigration station consisted of several wooden buildings, including a hospital, the Administration Building, and barracks for sleeping. The barracks were built to hold about 200 people. At times, as many as 500 people stayed there.

Waiting

When immigrants arrived on Angel Island, they were taken to the Administration Building. Officials separated men from the women and children. Each immigrant was checked for disease. People who would get well stayed at the hospital. People who would not get well were sent back to their homeland.

Immigrants who passed the health checkup were sent to the barracks. Metal bunks stacked three beds high filled the rooms. Sometimes as many as 200 people were packed into a room where there were supposed to be only 50 beds. Then the people waited.

Most immigrants did not speak English. Officials used interpreters to talk with immigrants who spoke a different language.

Tough Questions

When it was their turn, immigrants went to a hearing. U.S. officials asked detailed questions about the immigrants' lives and recorded the answers. Later, officials compared the answers with statements made by other family members. When answers didn't match, officials did not allow the person to enter the United States. Questioning lasted for days.

Most immigrants were held at Angel Island for about two or three days. Chinese immigrants often stayed for about three weeks. Some waited for months and even years to be let into the United States.

Officials asked difficult questions, such as "What is the name of the oldest man in your village?" and "Where is the well located in your village?" Many immigrants memorized hundreds of facts about their homes and villages before coming to Angel Island.

Words on a Wall

The long wait made many immigrants feel as if they were in jail. Barbed-wire fences and guards posted outside locked doors added to this feeling.

Some immigrants told about their sadness by writing or carving poems onto the walls. One person wrote, "For what reason must I sit in jail? It is only because my country is weak and my family is poor."

只是为我的祖国太弱。

我为什么坐牢

只是

While waiting, immigrants also read, wrote letters, listened to records, or washed clothes. Sometimes members of local churches brought sewing materials and gave women English language lessons.

Fire!

Over the years, people complained about the poor conditions and unsafe wooden buildings. When the Administration Building burned down in 1940, the government closed the Angel Island Immigration Station.

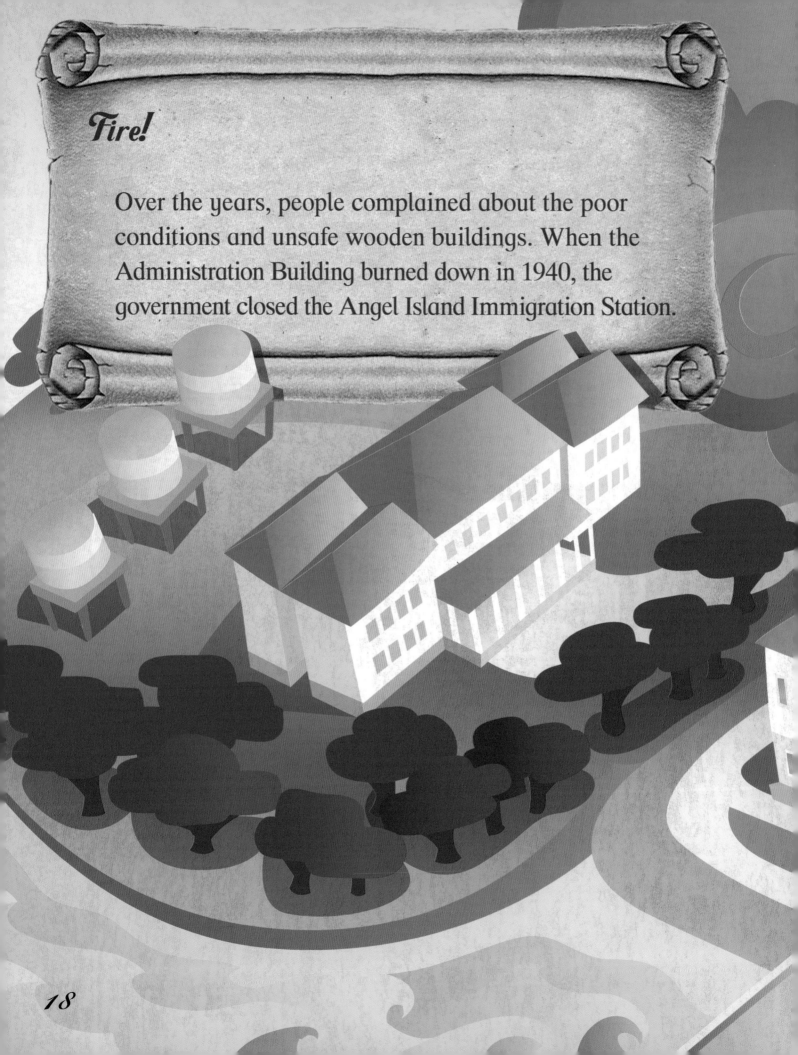

By then, the paperwork for 1 million immigrants had been processed at the Angel Island Immigration Station. The people included about 175,000 Chinese and 150,000 Japanese immigrants.

The following year, the U.S. Army began using the Angel Island Immigration Station as a place to process prisoners of war during World War II (1939–1945). After the war, the buildings were abandoned. In 1954, Angel Island became a California State Park.

By 1970, the government planned to destroy the remaining buildings. Before they were destroyed, Alexander Weiss, a park ranger, discovered the poems carved on the walls. He realized that the Angel Island Immigration Station was a part of American history and its people's struggle for freedom.

我为什么坐牢
只是因为我的国家弱
只是因为我的家里穷。

In 1943, government officials reversed the unfair Chinese Exclusion Laws. The United States became allies with China during World War II.

In 1997, the Angel Island Immigration Station was declared a National Historic Landmark. Today, people can visit a museum in the barracks. They can see the poems that were carved into the walls long ago. The next time you're in San Francisco, visit Angel Island. It is a symbol of hope for immigrants and their struggle for freedom.

Angel Island Facts

Angel Island
Immigration Station
in 1915

- In August 1775, Spanish explorer Juan Manuel de Ayala sailed into San Francisco Bay and saw an island. He named the island *Isla de Los Angeles* or "Island of the Angels" after the Catholic feast day of Our Lady of the Angels.

- Angel Island is the largest island in San Franscisco Bay. The state park covers 740 acres (296 hectares).

- Angel Island was known as the "Ellis Island of the West." Immigrants from nearly 90 different countries came through the Angel Island Immigration Station.

- While the Chinese Exclusion Laws were lifted in 1943, other laws restricting the number of Chinese immigrants were not lifted until 1965.

Glossary

barracks — a large plain building or group of buildings where many people live

California Gold Rush — (1848–1855) migration to the western United States when gold was discovered in California

citizen — someone who is a member of a particular country and who is protected by its laws; Chinese people could be U.S. citizens only if they were born in the United States

exclusion — the act of keeping something or someone out

immigrant — a person who leaves one country and settles in another

interpreter — a person who translates one language into another language to help people who speak different languages communicate

processed — put through a series of tasks

race — a group of people who share certain physical characteristics

World War II — (1939–1945) the war fought between the United States, Great Britain, France, and the Soviet Union against Germany, Japan, and Italy

To Learn More

More Books to Read

Brimner, Larry Dane. *Angel Island*. New York: Children's Press, 2001.

Currier, Katrina Saltonstall. *Kai's Journey to Gold Mountain*. Tiburon, Calif.: Angel Island Association, 2005.

Lee, Milly. *Landed*. New York: Farrar Straus Giroux, 2006.

On the Web

FactHound offers a safe, fun way to find Web sites related to topics in this book. All of the sites on FactHound have been researched by our staff.

1. Visit *www.facthound.com*
2. Type in this special code: 1404847049
3. Click on the FETCH IT button.

Your trusty FactHound will fetch the best sites for you!

Index

Look for all of the books in the American Symbols series:

Angel Island
The Bald Eagle
The Bill of Rights
Ellis Island
The Great Seal of the United States

The Liberty Bell
The Lincoln Memorial
Our American Flag
Our National Anthem
Our U.S. Capitol
The Pledge of Allegiance

The Statue of Liberty
Uncle Sam
The U.S. Constitution
The U.S. Supreme Court
The White House